SIMEON MOUNTAIN

Nulato

SIMEON MOUNTAIN

Nulato

SPIRIT MOUNTAIN PRESS

ISBN: 0-910871-05-1

Interviewing and Editing:
Yvonne Yarber and Curt Madison

Photography:
Curt Madison (unless otherwise noted)

Translations:
Eliza Jones (her translations in the text are followed by the initials E.J.) Courtesy of the Alaska Native Language Center, University of Alaska-Fairbanks.

Material collected September, 1979 and 1981 in
Nulato, Alaska.

Manuscript approved by Simeon Mountain, May, 1982.

SPIRIT MOUNTAIN PRESS
P.O. BOX 1214 FAIRBANKS, ALASKA 99707

Produced by:
Yukon-Koyukuk School District of Alaska

Regional School Board:
Donald Honea Sr. - Chairman
Pat McCarty - Vice Chairman
Eddie Bergman - Treasurer
Fred Lee Bifelt - Clerk
Luke Titus

Superintendent: Joe Cooper
Assistant superintendent: Fred Lau
Project Coordinator: Don Kratzer

Supplemental funding:
Johnson O'Malley Grant - EOOC14202516

**Library of Congress
Cataloging in Publication Data**

Madison, Curt
Yarber, Yvonne
Mountain, Simeon - Nulato. A Biography
YKSD Biography Series
ISBN 0-910871-05-1

1. Mountain, Simeon. 2. Koyukon-Athabaskan
3. Alaska Biography

Frontispiece:
Simeon's family in front of their home in Nulato, Alaska 1979. Front: Cletus Sipary Mountain; Row two: Vera and Marvin Mountain; Row three: Paul John, Kris Ann, Erick and Kevin Mountain; Row four: Simeon Sr., Josephine and Simeon Mountain, Jr.

A Note From a Linguist

As you read through this autobiography you will notice a style and a diction you may not have seen before in print. This is because it is an oral storytelling style. This autobiography has been complied from many hours of taped interviews. As you read you should listen for the sound of the spoken voice. While it has not been possible to show all the rhythms and nuances of the speaker's voice, much of the original style has been kept. If posssible you should read aloud and use your knowledge of the way the old people speak to recapture the style of the original.

This autobiography has been written in the original style for three reasons. First, the original style is kind of dramatic poetry that depends on pacing, succinctness, and semantic indirectness for its narrative impact. The original diction is part and parcel of its message and the editors have kept that diction out of a deep respect for the person represented in this autobiography.

The second reason for keeping the original diction is that it gives a good example of some of the varied richness of the English language. English as it is spoken in many parts of the world and by many different people varies in style and the editors feel that it is important for you as a reader to know, understand and respect the wide resources of this variation in English.

The third reason for writing in the original style is that this style will be familiar to many of you who will read this book. The editors hope that you will enjoy reading something in a style that you may never have seen written before even though you have heard it spoken many times.

Ron Scollon
Alaska Native Language Center
University of Alaska
Fairbanks
1979

Acknowledgements

Our thanks to the people who have helped continue this series. Ron Scollon and Eliza Jones of the University of Alaska for their help with language; Bea Hagen for typing transcripts; Cheryl DeHart for typing the final manuscript; the Manley Hot Springs Community School Committee for providing a place to work; Janis Carney and Liza Vernet for proofreading the final manuscript; Bob Maguire for inventing the idea and Joe Cooper, Fred Lau, and Mavis Brown for carrying out the administrative end of the project in Nenana; and to the Yukon-Koyukuk School District Regional Board who continue to support local curriculum.

And finally, thanks to Spirit Mountain Press: Larry Laraby, owner and chief headache man; Doug Miller, layout with an artistic flair; Eva Bee and her bear, who do much more than just typesetting; Judy Morris, layout apprentice and jack-of-all-trades.

All royalties from the sale of this book go to the Yukon-Koyukuk School District for the production of more autobiographies.

This is the first printing of this book. Please let us know about any corrections for future printings.

Foreword

This book is the thirteenth produced by the Yukon-Koyukuk School District in a series meant to provide cultural understanding of our own area and relevant role models for students. Too often Interior Alaska is ignored in books or mentioned only in conjunction with its mineral resources such as the gold rush or oil pipeline. We are gauged by what we are worth to Outside people. People living in the Interior certainly have been affected by those things but also by missionaries, wage labor, fur prices, celebrations, spring hunts, schools, technology, potlatches, and much more. For residents, Interior Alaska is all of those things people do together, whether in the woods, on the river, in the village or on Two Street. It's a rich and varied culture often glossed over in favor of things more easily written and understood.

This project was begun in 1977 by Bob Maguire. Representatives of Indian Education Parent Committees from each of Yukon-Koyukuk School District's eleven villages met in Fairbanks February of 1978 to choose two people from each village to write about. A variety of selection means were used—from school committees to village council elections. Despite the fact that most of the representatives were women, few women were chosen for the books. As the years passed, more women were added to give a more complete accounting of recent cultural changes.

It is our goal to provide a vehicle for people who live around us so they can describe the events of their lives in their own words. To be singled out as an individual as we have done in this series has not always been comfortable for the biographees, particularly for those who carry the strong Koyukon value of being humble. Talking about oneself has been a conflict overridden by the desire and overwhelming need to give young people some understanding of their own history in a form they have become accustomed to. A growing number of elders who can't read or write themselves think young people won't believe anything unless it's written in a book. This project attempts to give oral knowledge equal time in the schools.

As materials of this kind become more common, methods of gathering and presenting oral history get better. The most important ingredient is trust. After many hours of interview, people often relax to the point of saying some personal things they prefer left unpublished. After editing the tape transcripts we bring the rough draft manuscript back to the biographees to let them add or delete things before it becomes public. Too often those of us living in rural Alaska have been researched *on* or written *about* for an audience far away. This series is meant to bring information full round--from us back to us for our own uses.

Too many people in the Interior have felt ripped-off by journalists and bureaucrats. Hundreds pass through every year, all wanting information and many never to return. Occasionally their finished work may find its way back to the source only to flare emotions when people feel misrepresented. Perhaps a tight deadline or the lack of travel money may be the excuse for not returning for verification or approval. That is no consolation for people who opened up and shared something of themselves and are left feeling betrayed. We work closely with the biographees to check facts and intentions. The books need to be intimate and daring but the last thing we want to do is make someone's life more difficult. We need to share information in a wholesome way. After all, we're all in this together.

Comments about the biographies, their use, corrections, questions, or anything else is welcome.

Curt Madison
Yvonne Yarber
December 10, 1982
Manley Hot Springs
Alaska 99756

Table Of Contents

Introduction

Simeon Mountain, Sr. lives in Nulato, an Athabaskan village of about 300 people which was established in 1838 as a Russian trading post. Simeon grew up in Nulato strongly influenced both by the education he received at the Catholic mission and the old ways of his elders.

While Simeon can still speak the language of his ancestors, enjoys Athabaskan singing and dancing and follows some of the old customs, he is glad to have the convenience modern technology brings. He has traveled to far away places such as Rome, Japan and the Phillipines. And, as a postmaster, National Guard First Sargeant and taxi operator has taken advantage of modern transportation and communication systems.

As with others in Nulato, Simeon is a complex mixture of old ways and new. He is a business man and works on local politics. Between all the work, meetings and speeches however, he can always find the time for a game of chance with the cards. He has become famous for his "poker face" throughout the middle Yukon.

Local Area

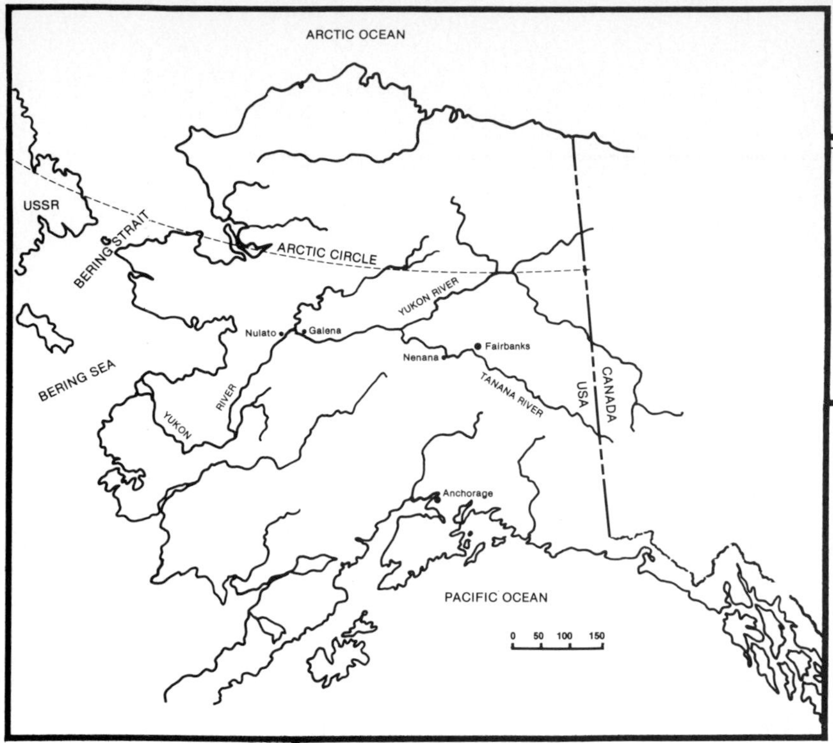

ARCTIC OCEAN

USSR

BERING STRAIT

ARCTIC CIRCLE

BERING SEA

YUKON RIVER

Nulato • • Galena • Fairbanks

Nenana

TANANA RIVER

YUKON RIVER

USA | CANADA

Anchorage

PACIFIC OCEAN

0 50 100 150

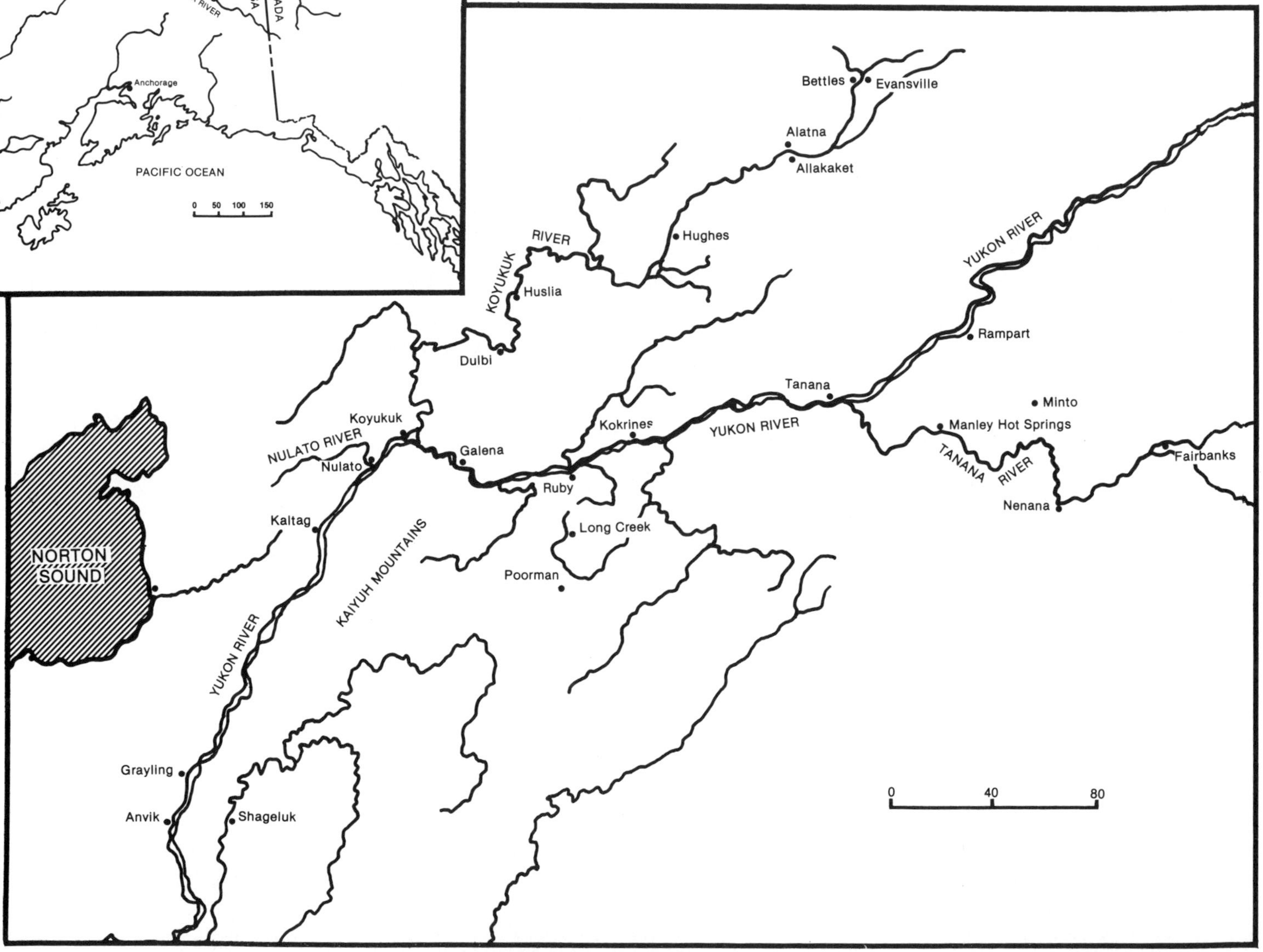

Bettles • Evansville

Alatna •

Allakaket

KOYUKUK RIVER

Hughes

YUKON RIVER

Huslia

Dulbi

Rampart

Tanana

Minto •

Koyukuk

Kokrines

Manley Hot Springs

NULATO RIVER

Nulato

Galena

YUKON RIVER

Ruby

TANANA RIVER

Fairbanks

Kaltag

Long Creek

Nenana

NORTON SOUND

Poorman

KAIYUH MOUNTAINS

YUKON RIVER

Grayling

Anvik

Shageluk

0 40 80

10

Chapter One: We Never Went Hungry

Christmas Stockings

The first Christmas I remember I was living with my mother. Christmas Eve it was. Tomorrow was going to be Christmas. Before we went to bed I see her writing on paper or something like that. I thought to myself she was writing to Santa Claus. My brother, Cosmos, Jr., and I went to bed and next morning when we woke up I think we found this on the table. Two little mouth organs and a little tiny ball. I thought that was what Santa Claus brought. I thought Mom was writing to Santa Claus the night before and that was how these things came.

Then the next Christmas I remember. I started to go to school. Maybe I was six or seven. I remember I hear kids talking about hanging up stockings. Well, I thought there was really a Santa Claus those days. So I hung up a stocking. I was living at my aunt and uncle's at that time. Daniel and Jessie Sipary. I hung up stockings over the bed. I couldn't sleep that night. Think to catch Santa Claus coming in.

You know, I finally fell asleep. Early next morning, when I woke up, the first thing, I opened my eyes and looked up at the socks over my bed. We had lines then, far up along the ceiling to dry clothes. That's where I had hung up the stockings. It was still hanging in the way I hung it up. I was very disappointed.

Since then I knew there wasn't a Santa Claus. I don't know.

Cyprian Peter, Liza Peter Johnson and Simeon Mountain Sr., in Nulato, 1939.

Maybe my aunt and uncle didn't see it. Maybe I didn't hang it up right. Anyway, we didn't have very much money. But we never went hungry. One thing you know.

When I was growing up you go to different houses and sometimes see people eating only one dish. Just like fish or meat with tea. I used to see that. And nothing else with it. Although my Uncle Dan didn't have very much money, we always had two or three things with the fish. Like maybe fish and macaroni and cheese, or rice, potatoes. Fruit sometimes. And other greens. So I was never hungry in that part.

Dad and Mom

I was born May 11, 1932, up Koyukuk River. Dulbi. I guess my mom and dad were up there for the spring, trying to catch muskrats. I guess I belong to Koyukuk River. I grow up most around Nulato and Kaiyuh. But you know Edwin Simon from Huslia. He died you know. He was very active in everything. He used to always tell me that I belong to Koyukuk River. If I was around people from other villages he used to embarrass me in front of them. He used to introduce me as from Koyukuk River. He used to tell them, "That's the reason we're trying to get him back. Only smart people come out of the Koyukuk River."

I don't remember my dad. He died of heart attack when I was one, maybe two years old. I only know what people tell me. I guess they got his name from the Bible. Cosmos Mountain. He was a good carpenter. Houses. Cupboards, tables, and he used to do a lot of fancy work. Maybe make flowers or

Oregon Province Jesuit Archives

L-R: Lucille Mountain standing in front and held by her mother Vivian Peter, Simeon Mountain, Sr. in overalls and Simel Peter holding Flora (Peter) Esmailka. Nulato, late 1930's.

kinds of designs and he never used to go to school for it. Just learned by himself. And no electric tools in those days.

I heard someone from Galena here in Nulato last night. Jimmy Malemute. I was sitting down and he was playing this violin. He said that my dad used to be the best violin player. He's the one who taught him and Justin Patsy. They used to go see him and ask him to teach them how to play. So they used to sit with him and they learned how.

Another thing, he was good in sports. I always hear people talk about it. He was good in baseball. In those days they

Vivian Peter, Nulato 1982.

Vivian Peter, grandson, and Simel Peter, Nulato 1982.

13

used to play hardball. Not softball like we play now. This Father Mac (McElmeel) taught them how to play. They used to have a good team here in Nulato. None of the villages could beat them.

My mom is still living, Vivian. Vivian Peters. She's remarried. First I lived with mom. For a while I was going back and forth between my uncle and my mom. Around eight or nine years old I started staying with my uncle and aunt for good. But when I was with my mom, we stayed below Kaltag. Maybe about thirty miles. The name of the place is "Behind the Island."

I remember one fall my stepdad, Simel Peters, was trapping. One time I told Josephine, my wife, I thought I dreamt something. We were somewhere. My mom, I remember my mom and she was carrying a baby. There were four of us. We were standing on land and there was water all around us. I told Josephine a few times about it. She told mom, and mom told her that was in 1937 flood. My uncle, Dan Sipary, was the only one that had a boat. He was shuttling people to higher ground. We were the last ones to get evacuated from Kaiyuh.

Springtime, the whole town used to go up the Kaiyuh. Silas, McGinty's, Stickman's, Saunder's, almost everyone. And at every camp there used to be two, three families. One thing I didn't like about ours, we were always alone. One family. I used to be lonesome. I want to stay in one of the other camps with two or three families so we could play with other children. But sometimes we would visit each other, hunting and stuff like that. Used to be a lot of fun.

The McGinty and Saunders' families were at Nine Mile cutting wood just like us. The whole family used to cut wood for

the boats. *Steamer Nenana* and *Alice*, all those big boats.
Maybe we had contract to cut twenty, thirty, forty, fifty cords
maybe. In the fall and all winter. Then in springtime, the boat
would land at those woodpiles. They used it for fuel to keep
the boats running.

In our family was my uncle and aunt, Daniel and Jessie
Sipary, there was Ivan, Winnie, Priscilla, Edward, myself, and
Janet, our adopted sister. They were all too small, most of the
time it used to be just Uncle and I cutting wood. Janet used to
help a little, getting branches away from the tree. The others
were too small for two-man saw. Are you familar with two-
man saw? They're about five feet long.

Spring Muskrats

We used to go out in the spring you know. On the crust.
Most of the time we used to walk. My adopted sister Janet and
I used to start three or four o'clock in the morning. Walking
two or three hours ahead of my uncle and aunt. We used to
enjoy running across the river and running and walking all the
way on the Kaiyuh Trail. They catch us up around Dinner
Camp. That's about halfway between here and Kaiyuh. After
they caught us up, there was no place for us to ride on the sled.
So we had to run and walk trying to keep up with them. All
the way to Kaiyuh. Maybe fifteen to twenty miles. We didn't
think nothing of it.

We used to stay up there for three weeks. Altogether get
maybe two, three hundred muskrat. Most the time we come
out the last week of May. Come out by boats, by Kaiyuh

Slough. Used to be quite a sight, four, five, six families coming out in six, seven boats maybe, and only one inboard pushing it all. We would have to tie up to them cause we had only a rowboat. People pay in those days, about ten, fifteen dollars for towing you out.

It used to be a lot of fun. Most of the time we travel night and day. It would take two days and a night. The men relieve each other steering. Only one person had to steer the boat and another person would be way out in the other boat where you couldn't make the real quick bends. He'd have to hit it with a paddle. And we'd stop once or twice during the trip to make tea. Everybody eat. But a lot of times you just keep going and people eat in the boat.

Sometimes there would be other groups of boats. We used to wait at Two Mile till all the boats caught up with each other. Then we all come right behind each other coming to town. Soon as we leave Two Mile we start shooting shotgun and rifle. All the people that are in town, they answer us. It sound good.

I remember one of the Sisters, her first year here, during the Second World War. She didn't know what was going on every spring when the people come out of the Kaiyuh. Early one morning around four o'clock she start hearing a lot of shooting. She got scared. Ran to the next room to wake the other Sisters, telling them the Japs are coming. Here it was Kaiyuh people, coming out.

Sometimes we used to have to make camp at the mouth of Kaiyuh Slough when the river was rough. But when you're coming out of Kaiyuh Slough and it's not too rough, even if you're hungry you don't want to stop there. You want to keep on going. You want to get to this side of the river before the

16

wind comes up. You want to get home as soon as you could. While it's calm.

When everyone get home from Kaiyuh, you pack up all your spring outfit, clean up your houses and dance. Mostly dancing and drinking. In the older days I think they used to gamble a lot with muskrats, traps, bullets and matches. But not very often in my time. After all the dancing they get ready for fishing.

Nulato 1914. Unidentified man making a split spruce funnel for a fishtrap tied with willow bark or roots. Later traps were made of wire.

Manook in winter garb.

Fishing

I remember a story my grandpa, Charlie Mountain, used to tell about my dad and uncle, Daniel Sipary, when they were young. They just got married, maybe two or three years. They used to really like each other. Brother-in-laws, he never saw any brother-in-law like that. They really thought a lot of each other.

One time they moved to camp. There was nothing at the camp. They pitched up the tent and started to work. They bet each other, to see who was going to last the longest without sleep. They just started to work. They started to make wheel first. They finished the wheel, built the smokehouse, and the fish racks. By that time they had set the wheel and everything. It was time to cut fish. They had worked three days and three nights. Around the clock without sleeping. The third day around noon, they started cutting fish.

My grandpa and grandma were telling me. They go to bed at night, you know, my grandpa and grandma. The next morning when they get up my dad and Uncle Dan is still working. So this third day, Grandpa say it's just like he don't see my uncle around. Grandpa looked under the fish rack and here he saw him passed out right on the rocks. The slime from the fish was just dripping down in his face. Three days and three

Daniel Sipary and his uncle, Manook in Nulato.

18

nights without sleeping.

My Uncle Dan was the best friend I ever had. Remember when I talk about going back and forth between the two families. I didn't mind it. First, I want my mom. After I got used to it, it didn't bother me. I didn't want to leave my uncle. I remember how I cried when he died of cancer around '58 or '59.

My uncle wasn't a hunter, so I more or less had to learn by myself and from other people. My uncle was a fisherman. And I think it's better. I wish I had his skills. Because now to fish year round, you'll never get hungry. But with the hunting,

Adam Minook's fishtrap near Tanana.

19

a lot of times you'll come home skunked. Especially when you have to feed a family. He used to work a fishwheel. Fishtrap. Fresh fish all year around. Not one kind, you know, grayling, lush, trout, sheefish, and little greasy whitefish.

I should tell you how we used to get them. In the fall, September, we put in fish trap across the Nulato River. All the way across. Now it's against the law and we could put the fishtrap only halfway. We cannot block the whole river. In those days we used to block the whole river.

The trap was small wire, maybe five or six feet long and a little funnel in the front. We used to face it upriver right in the riffles. Put in pegs all the way and willows against it. Then the fish would be facing upriver, just like swimming but they're drifting down. They go into the fishtrap tail first. We catch them *sil yee lookk'a'* in White man way we call them little skinny whitefishes. Then we used to catch trout, grayling and lush. We have Indian name for them too, but it would take me time to remember them. So, that's falltime.

Then, later on in the winter, around February, we put in fishtrap out in the Yukon. A bigger one. We used to catch lush, sheefish, whitefish and little whitefish. Not the same kind of little whitefish in the Nulato River. These ones are about the same size, but they're fatter and they're greasy. What we call them in Indian is just on my tongue now, *dilmiga*.

To put in a fishtrap is a lot of work out in the river. In Nulato River it's easy, but out in the Yukon, no. First you got to go out in the woods and find a big tree that'll split easy. Into little sticks. I used to see him working way late at night. Midnight, two o'clock sometimes. Sitting down on the floor splitting these things. Lot of patience. That's the only thing I think that would get me stuck to put in fishtrap. I think about it a lot of times. I'm sure I could put one in. Because after I got a little older my uncle used to just like let me direct the operations. I used to be the eye-man.

There's certain way you have to put down those poles for the trap to go between. It has to be perfect or you'll have trouble all the time. The fence is nothing, you can put your poles in any old way. But putting in fishtrap takes a lot of work, a lot of time and a lot of patience.

During the winter most of the fish was for food. We never used it for dogs. My uncle used to sell a lot of fish cheap. Sometimes he'd sell only to certain people even if there was lots of fish. He wouldn't sell to people who feed fresh fish and bones leftovers to the dogs. You'd have to wait because next time there'd be no fish if you feed fresh fish to dogs. There was a pilot used to come in here. He put in order and haul them back to Fairbanks. I guess he resold them. I don't know. Whitefish and sheefish but not too much lush. So we ate a lot of fish when I was growing up. I didn't mind because it was all different and fresh. It's not like going to your freezer right now. It doesn't taste the same.

Nobody use trap in winter now. A few people put in fishnet and get whitefish and sheefish in the Yukon. In the fall, we put in hooks out on the ice. Last fall we did and caught a few lush. Put in big bait hook with a piece of fish on it. Maybe ten hooks on a line and string a line under the ice. Lot of people did that last fall. I'm going to do that again this year.

Then in summer, we'd have fishwheel. We catch whitefish, dog salmon, king salmon. Not very much king salmon. Mostly silvers and chinook salmons. My uncle never used

Boats on the banks of the Yukon, Nulato 1982.

21

fishnet. Only fishtraps and fishwheel.

All our lives, up until a few years before uncle died, we never had no inboard or out-board. We used to walk, pulling the boat two and a half miles upriver. Every morning. Hot sun. Two people. One in the boat and one walking, pulling. I was the younger, so I used to walk. I let my uncle steer.

I got to where I used to hate that walk two and a half miles, pulling a rowboat. Then we put 500 fish in the boat and row back down. All arm power.

For a while we had couple dogs that were pretty good. They were pulling us, like pull-

Marie (Mountain) Dayton at the Mountain's fish camp, 1977.

Simeon Mountain Collection

ing a sled. They walk along the beach with harness on them. You sit in the boat and have a free ride. Dog has to be really good for that. Then when you get to the fishwheel, you have to row real hard around it. The current was strong. Now all you got to do is get in the boat and pull the kicker. Take off. Sometimes I enjoy walking with boat but sometimes I used to say to myself, I'm going to buy kicker first chance I get. I did. Around 1960, after I got married.

22

Hunting Accident

My uncle and aunt never used to want me to go hunting. Never wanted me to handle gun. They were always afraid of an accident. I guess one of the main reasons my other uncle, I don't know him, was shot by accident. My Uncle Dan's brother Edward. His favorite brother. I guess everybody's favorite. I hear people talk about him a lot of times.

Up on the Kaiyuh, they were hunting rabbits. You know how people will line up and walk through the woods. Chase rabbits to a point of an island or somewhere. When they get to the point of the island, all the rabbits will be there and everybody shoot. That's how my uncle was shot. He was very young too. Maybe twenty.

Another person was shot too doing that. People say that he didn't holler anything. They heard a shot and he fell to his knees. He just said, "God have mercy," or something like that, and he died. My Uncle Edward bled to death. They shot him in the leg. He lost all his blood coming down the Kaiyuh. I guess that was the reason why they never wanted me to handle gun.

We hunt rabbits once in a while now. Across the island. A whole bunch of us. But everybody uses shotguns. So there's no danger. Just as long as you're not pointing at someone. We don't use .22 because they glance, riquochet off things. Shotgun just goes into the ground.

I think last time we did that was two or three years ago. There was 12 or 15 of us, everybody keep what they catch, which usually isn't very much. One or two each. Maybe we got ten in the group. One of the men got one alive. He saw it run inside of little snow bank. Put his hand in, grabbed it. Wasn't shot.

Oregon Province Jesuit Archives, photo by Father Jetté

Edward Sipary

Moose Hunting

Right off when I started hunting moose, I started being lucky. That made Uncle worry for quite a while because it's no good. In our Indian way it's no good when you're too lucky. People say you're not going to do that for long. You wouldn't be around long if you were too lucky. In anything. No, sometimes it's good to be a little out of luck I guess. I was just teenager and it didn't bother me. Before uncle died, he was telling me to teach my cousins how to hunt. They're just like my brothers. I was raised with them.

The way I learn is figure it out I guess. You go out and hunt. After you hunt for a while you can tell. Moose tracks especially the ones you want to watch out for. You can tell whether they're fresh or a day old, or two days old, or this morning. Common sense, like whether the moose crossed before the snow, during the snow, or after the snow. Then too you have to take wind and stuff into consideration. You don't want to walk with the wind because if they smell, they take off right now. Check if there's lake, clearing, a lot of times you'll see moose. Only lucky people drive right up to it, where you don't have to work packing it. Sometimes we have to pack moose a long ways.

One of the first ones I got, we were hunting up on the Yukon, Bishop's Slough. Right across from Bishop Mountain. Three of us were hunting. Ivan, my younger brother, and Ray Ambrose, my good friend who drowned up across the river. Three of us didn't know very much about hunting. So using inboard we went down Bishop's Slough less than a mile. It was getting dark, so we wanted to camp around there. We stopped in this one place, looked like it was a dry creek.

We started walking up this dry creek. I was ahead of them. After we walked quarter of a mile I saw some kind of old tracks coming toward the dry creek. I say to myself, well, they might be coming from a lake.

24

Even though the tracks is old, I'll follow to see where they came from. I kept following the old tracks into the woods. Pretty soon I started coming into an opening, like it started getting daylight. It was a small lake. I sneak up slowly. Stop once in a while. Pretty soon I saw a moose. Cow moose. I got pretty close to it by that time.

I didn't see the bull. They always say, be careful, you're supposed to get the bull before the cow. Cows was open too in those days. While I was taking two or three steps I looked so I wouldn't step on twigs and make noise. The cow moose was looking at me already. I made three or four steps and looked up again. I saw that bull walk right in front of the cow, covered the cow. I don't know where it came from. I took a deep breath and shot at it. The bull fell down. The cow started to run. I shot at it. I thought I hit it but wasn't sure. Anyway, I waited there for a while and Ivan and Ray came back to me. We just gut the bull because it was getting dark. We made camp.

Next morning, we butchered it and packed it out. I tell them, "Let's go, let's walk around to see if we'll find the cow. I shot at it. We don't want to kill it for nothing." I showed them where I shot at it. It bled for a while and then there was no more blood. We just walked anyplace in the woods in the direction it was facing. We came to it about a mile back. They shot it again and we packed it all out.

After we got all through we brought all the meat right near the boat. All we got to do is throw it in the boat. Another moose came out! It was right there. They wanted to kill it but I told them no. We were allowed one moose each, but I didn't want. We didn't have enough room in the boat and besides, ice started to run.

To tell you how much we knew about hunting, all that time we were living on sun-dry fish. We eat two sun-dry fish for breakfast, two sun-dry fish for lunch, same thing for supper. Here we didn't know all you got to do is cut the moose meat and put it on a stick, cook yourself some meat.

To me, hunting moose never changed since those days. Except it is much easier for you to travel long ways now with the outboard. In those days you had inboard and it was hard to go up side creeks and over sandbars. Otherwise the hunting part is the same.

Joy

I thought I would never have dogs after I got old enough. We had about ten and I used to have to feed them every night. I didn't enjoy it. Long time ago I used to say I'd never have dogs. There was no reason for me to have dogs because when I was twenty-one I went into the army. When I got out, two years later I became a postmaster. All these years I've had only two dogs. I had one for fifteen years maybe. It died last April. I sure didn't want to lose it. It was a good hunting dog. He used to stop moose for me.

There's a few in town like that. Not very many. Usually how they learned was to go out with the other dogs. If they do it once, that's all it takes. Next time they know how to go about it. This dog learned by itself.

Joy. We used to call it Joy. Went out with me one time. It saw a moose, ran in front of it and he held it. That was all. I didn't think nothing about it. Two years after that I took him out with a friend of mine, Fabian George. It started following him. Pretty soon I heard him shoot. I went to him and he had a moose. He said the dog stopped it. After that I believed it.

Sometimes you start walking. Pretty soon you come to fresh tracks and keep walking. This dog used to warn you. I used to hear people say a lot of dogs do that but I never believed it. When we get close to moose the dog comes back. Wait. Then it run toward the moose and come back again. I guess the dog is saying go faster. After a while you hear it barking. Sure enough, it had the moose. Just walk to it and shoot it.

Vivian Peter's parents Olga and Joseph, known as Mr. and Mrs. Onion. Standing in front are Lily Stickman and Lily Esmailka.

Chapter Two: Long Time Ago

Grandma and Grandpa Mountain

I remember my grandma and grandpa very good, but it's hard for me to think of certain stories to tell. There are things about them that I would like my children and grandchildren to know. I guess it was before my grandpa and grandma's time, they used to live underground. Maybe you hear about that. They used to call them *naahuloo yah*. I have hard time to pronounce it. All it means is underground houses. They dig into the ground and have a little hole up in the ceiling where the smoke will go through when they have a fire. In grandpa's days they started living in log cabins.

I remember grandpa used to say, when they were growing up out camp, their parents let them run without shoes. Pick wood and stuff like that. So they would get tough I guess. Even in winter. In those days people make their living mostly by trapping, fishing and hunting. There wasn't moose. The moose started to come when grandpa was a teenager or a little older. They lived only on caribou, rabbits, chickens, ducks and so forth. There used to be a lot of caribou around here in his younger days. They all moved away. I don't know why. Then the moose came. They hunted a lot with bow and arrow. Birch, sinew for the string, sharp objects for the point of the arrow. They used to kill big game. People talk about grandpa. He used to shoot the ducks down in the air with bow and arrow. People now with shotgun miss a lot. Few years ago I saw a young boy with bow and arrow but people here aren't much involved in it. I saw one in the catalog the other day that cost about two hundred fifty dollars. If a person learned how to use it I think it would be a good way to hunt. You wouldn't make no noise so you could get quite a few shots.

I remember one story about grandpa. In those days they used to wear suits. Suit of clothes. Now they don't. Someone was telling me about Indian people selling wood to steamboat. They were trying to talk to the captain. This White guy working on the steamboat with suit of clothes. White shirt, red tie. Well, these Indian people can't understand the captain. They were having hard time to make some kind of a deal. They don't understand the price or anything.

They got happy when they saw my grandpa dressed up like a White man. They went up to him and told him in their language, ''We are glad to see you, you can talk for us.''

My grandpa look at them and said, ''Gee, I don't even know how to say give me water in English.'' If that story was told in Indian, it sounds more funnier.

Lot of the old ways I learned from my grandma and grandpa. A lot of things we used to do they tell us, ''*hutlanee.*'' In our language means, it's no good to do that. Everything used

Kooyhghaneeda, *Vivian Peter's grandmother. Nulato 1913.*

to be *hut*I*anee*. I cannot express the meaning of it in English. *Hut*I*anee* to me sounds like it's no good, or maybe you wouldn't live long. Something like that.

It's the way I was telling you, I used to be lucky. Well, that's *hut*I*anee*. I remember them warning us when we ate fresh fish not to run around. Not to play ball. *Hut*I*anee* to run around after we ate fresh fish. In those days we used to play football right out there in the road. Everybody, young and old. Good exercise. Used to play way into dark, until seven o'clock, wintertime.

Another thing we never used to do is feed dogs fresh fish bones or leftovers from supper. You have to wait until the next evening. I don't know the reason. It was just *hut*I*anee*. No good.

So lot of the old people forbid their children to eat certain food. Like the best part. They want it for themselves I guess. They used to warn teenage girls when they're twelve on up not to eat certain part of beaver. They say they'll have a hard time to have children. In our language we call it *misteeghon*. It's hipbone of the beaver. Even now, we observe it. Well, we don't believe it, but we still tell our girls not to eat it. That part. Otherwise they eat everything we cook.

We don't observe the other rules anymore. Like after you eat fresh fish. We just don't do it.

Drawing by Father Baud. Oregon Province Jesuit Archives.

Simeon's grandparents, Charlie and Mary Mountain at their fish camp outside of Nulato. Circa 1950.

Wars

Grandpa used to tell me stories. He used to tell us *huloyh*. In our language means a long time ago story. Most of them were true. I used to sit down and listen to him. To remember those things I have to sit down and think about it. That's been at least thirty-five years ago. I never think about it all that time.

I remember one story about the last time either the Koyukuk people or the Koyukuk River people came down to fight with us. I hear a lot of stories about it. We didn't know they were going to come. But there was a medicine man in Kaiyuh and he knew that something was going to happen. I believe it was his son or his son-in-law, middle age man the way they describe him, was coming down to Nulato from Kaiyuh. Nulato was down here about half a mile at that time. The name of the place is *Gazaalma*, we still call it *Gazaalma* (a Russian loan word meaning barracks, E.J.). Our village used to be there. Anyway, he was coming down from Kaiyuh and this medicine man had a feeling something might happen so he gave his underwear to his son to use.

Nulato, May 1982 showing trails, lake, airport, graveyard and old village.

He put it on and came down. I guess he was sleeping in a smokehouse. He start hearing noises. He realized that people came to fight with Nulato people. To kill them all. To burn them out. They were throwing grass inside and blocking the underground houses with sleds and lighting them.

This son starts feeling the wall inside the smokehouse. It's all upright logs. He finally came to one log that was loose. Easy, he pulled it apart and squeezed through there. They had all the snowshoes on one cache. Used to be all the caches one side. He was crawling. Sneaking to those caches like a dog so they wouldn't recognize him. He went up to the cache, reached up and grabbed a pair of snowshoes. He didn't know it was one side man's snowshoes, and the other side was woman's. He crawled into the woods and started walking back.

Out here somewhere there's a lake *Gazaalma*. He got on the trail and started running. Pretty soon he saw all these men standing on both sides of the trail. He watched them a long time. They never moved so he realized it was just parkas. They did that so nobody will escape. Just put parkas on both sides of the trail. He ran down around Two Mile and start running across the river. It was dark, in the winter. Halfway across the river they saw him. They said the light was so bright you could see way on the other side of the

Caches alongside Nulato cabins, 1982.

32

Nulato cemetary, 1982.

river. The light from the underground houses burning.

He heard them saying, "He's getting away." They sent two best runners after him. When he was getting on the other side of the river the runners were getting pretty close. He hear them talking together, "We don't know what he's going to do after he get back up there. Let's go back and tell the chief that we killed him." That way he was the only guy that escaped from that battle.

He made it back up the Kaiyuh next day. He told the people up there and they got ready for second war. The women were

33

making sinews, the men were making bows and arrows. They made something like a fort and they waited. Nobody came.

Another time we paid them back. We went up and did the same thing. I don't know where the town was, someplace up Koyukuk River, Nulato people did the same thing. They blocked up all their houses. Nobody could escape. There was one person there from Nulato. They told him to come out. "We want only you."

"No, I wouldn't come out without my wife," he said.

"We don't want your wife, we want only you," they keep telling him.

He says, "Go ahead, burn us. Burn all of us. I'll go with my wife." Finally they told him okay. So he came out with his wife and they burnt the whole town.

I hear stories about long time ago. Men never used to go out when they hear noises. Dogs barking or anything like that. Only the young girls or women used to go out and check what the dogs are barking for. I guess they were scared of war. And the enemy, it would be hard for them to kill a woman I guess. So only girls or women used to go out after dark to check different kind of noises.

Medicine People

Another time Koyukuk people came down. They picked only on the medicine man. They beat him and beat him and beat him up with a big club, I guess. Keep hitting him. I don't know how long they hit him and the tree keep glancing off of him. Just like hitting iron. Finally he start getting soft. After I don't know how long they finally killed him. They didn't touch nobody else. Then they all left, went back upriver, not one of them made it back to Koyukuk. They all froze. I guess the medicine man made such a strong medicine that not one of them made it back to Koyukuk. They all froze to death.

There was hardly any medicine people in Nulato since I start remembering. Those was before our days. I heard that when the missionaries came, they were against them. Told them not to practice. Since I start remembering we had only one old woman that was a medicine woman. Anna Stickman, mother of Fred Stickman who just died. His father was a pretty big medicine man.

Once I was hurt. I don't know how. I told my aunt and she had this Anna Stickman come. I didn't want her on account of my religion. She came by one evening and spit in her hand and rub it in my chest under my clothes. Rub it like that for a couple days. It went away. Never bother me no more.

People say my grandpa was a little bit medicine man too, but I never saw him making medicine. All the medicine people died off and nobody replaced them. People talk about it sometimes. They say maybe God allowed it because there was no doctors in those days. As there started being more doctors and nurses they gradually died off. The medicine man didn't pass it on.

I hear when they first started becoming medicine man, they'd get off their minds. Then they wake up in the middle of a fire and just walk out of it. They're okay after that. They used to do that so many times before they became medicine man or medicine woman.

I was afraid. My cousin, Elmer Manook, in Anchorage, he's like my brother. We were all raised together. He used to get like that in our teenage days. He used to disappear. I think even while he's standing among us. We go searching for him. We find him different places. Like in the cache, or in another house under somebody's bed, sleeping. We'd wake him up and he wouldn't know what happened.

He used to tell me that he might become a medicine man and he prayed a lot. So he wouldn't become a medicine man. After he got older it never bothered him. He got out of it. I remember that so well. For a while I thought he was going to become a medicine man too.

We didn't want to become medicine man in my days. My belief would be if I became a medicine man I would go below after I died. They claim some medicine people used to do a lot of wicked things. Like people would see a medicine man and tell him, "Well, that guy over there, I don't like him. Here's a piece of meat. Here's twenty dollars. Here's a fox skin. Do something about it." That person would pass away in a short time after. But if you do that they say a lot of times it turns back on you. Either you or your immediate family. If you went to see a medicine man and wished someone bad luck, later on it would turn back on you.

Even now people worry that a medicine man's spirit might still be around. We warn each other, especially the younger people when they go to other villages a long ways aways. Watch out how you talk. Don't laugh at people that look funny or crippled. Don't make any kind of remarks. It's *hutłanee*. But I don't know if there's any more medicine people.

Chapter Three: Nulato Mission

Oregon Province Jesuit Archives, Photo by Jetté

Front: Phillip Ambrose, Michael Silas; Back: Theodore Agnes, Johnny Warner, Frank Ambrose, Daniel Sipary in Nulato.

School

We used to cut wood down Ten Mile and come up to Nulato sometime in November. It would be December, January, February, March and then middle of April we go to Kaiyuh. That would be maybe five months out of the year we would go to school. Our family. Not every family. Some of them would be out at the trapline.

We never had school board or anything like that in those days. The Mission run the school. Nulato Mission. In the old days the Mission didn't have very much money. Compared to the school now. I heard when they first started the school it was just the four walls, a table, a bench and a few books. When I went to school we had long tables and benches that seat anywhere from four to six students on one bench. We all used the table.

My uncle and mother went to school there. My uncle could read and write. There's not too many like that in his age group. And he encouraged us to go to school while we were in town. There was other children that missed school. They sleep in. Their parents leave them alone. I never missed school. But a lot of times I wanted to be out.

I went to school till I was seventeen. The subjects in those days was mostly reading, writing and math. In math I used to get straight A's all the time. I always been good in math. I had hard time in English. Hard time with vowels, consonants, periods, commas, those things. I guess because we didn't have books, we had a hard time to learn. Especially reading. I only went as far as sixth grade. I was in that one grade for about three years. It only went to six grades in my time. After me, it went to eight grades.

There might have been thirty-five or forty of us altogether in each classroom. It was two classrooms. On one side it was the first to fourth grades. The other side was fifth, sixth and seventh. Catholic school. Sisters of St. Ann was our teachers.

I remember Sister Mary Pious, one of my teachers, always used to tell me, "Empty vessels made the most noise." I used to be wild. I wasn't very smart in school. I used to poke the girls as they passed by with a needle. Not hard. Just enough to make them squeal. Or I'd throw them a piece of paper or pencil or pinched them. I really liked to pinch them and Sister Mary Pious used to slap me. I just had a lot of life. One of my boys is like that. They say at school everytime some little boy or girl pass him, they scream. I guess he's doing the same thing I used to. I often wonder if Sister Mary Pious was here, what she'd say. I think I went a long ways since those days. All the things I have to do. Like working in the post office.

School is different today. We never used to have student travel. I see those kids running, playing basketball, even boxing during school hours. We never used to

Nulato children with Father Desjardins. Front row: unidentified; Second row: 1. Olga Nicholai, 2. unidentified, 3. Annunciata, 4. Charlie Brush, 5 and 6 unidentified, 7. Irene Demoski, 8. unidentified; Third row: 1. Theodore Agnes, 2. Joe Wiseman, 3. Andrew Johnson, 4. unidentified, 5. Fred Stickman, 6. Daniel Sipary, 7. Bernard Alexie; Back standing: 1. Teresa Glass, 2. unidentified, 3. Father Desjardins.

have P.E. After school we played hockey. We used a willow for the stick, bend it at the bottom. We used a little ball and play out here on the road fall and winter. Spring and any free time during summer months we played baseball.

Kids sit and watch television now after school. They don't go out and play very much. Most people in Nulato have television. Some have two. We have one downstairs and one

Boys working on Mission garden in Nulato, circa 1910. L-R: Theodore Agnes, Bernard Alexie, Andrew Johnson, Joe Wiseman.

upstairs. I try to tell the children to watch only one at a time because our electric bill go up to $300 a month. Lot of money, about thirty-four or forty-two cents per kilowatt hour.

I think there used to be more work for kids in our days. Feeding dogs. Cutting wood. Packing wood. Even have to haul wood. Haul water. Now it is much easier. A lot of people have trucks or sno-goes. The older people get through doing all these things while the children are in school, so the children have more free time then they did a long time ago.

In our days, fall and winter, all the school kids used to pack in wood for the school. Half an hour a day. It would be cut. My Uncle Dan worked for the Mission for fifty cents an hour, four dollars a day just cutting wood. That's maybe thirty years ago, not very long. Now people work for maybe ten or fifteen dollars an hour. The Youth Corps gets five dollars an hour. That's just young people.

Lot of times in the winter we haul a sled with our neck, water cans inside. We used to get the water from out in the river. We cut ice too. Right out in the river we used to cut a hundred or two hundred blocks per family to last all winter. The Mission had ice even in the summer, the clinic too. They used to have little buildings, we call icehouses. Insulated with sawdust. No one puts ice away for the summer now. Everybody has freezers.

About fifteen years ago we quit using the Yukon River water. People warn us it's not very good to drink because people up river throw things in the water. Then we'd go down one mile below town to the Nulato River. We used dogs or pay someone with dogs or sno-go. About five years ago we got this big Safe Water. The Council gives the water free but a lot of people couldn't get used to the chemicals. A lot of people still go to Nulato River or Mukluk Slough for their water.

Anyway, I was telling you about school and the Sisters of St. Ann. They used to tell us not to talk in Indian when we were going to school so we didn't. They warned us we'd get punished. Anyway, a lot of the students in my age group didn't understand Indian. There was just a few that spoke it. I can speak pretty good. My parents always speak Indian at home. But the missionaries told our parent's group the same thing. Not to talk Indian. Now the schools are encouraging bilingual.

It's a good idea to get it back again before it die away. I'm for teaching the language and the customs. I should talk to my children a little more often in Indian. They can speak some words and understand some things. When we had bilingual four or five years ago, the children would come home and say a lot of words. They surprised me sometimes. But now we don't have enough money for bilingual. They usually teach January to May, one hour a day. It isn't enough. My wife, Josephine, is one of the ones teaching bilingual.

The way I see it, in my days we were drifting farther and farther away from our language. We quit talking as much as we should. Our parents used to warn us not to talk our language when we're with people that don't understand because the other people might think we're talking about them.

Missionaries

It's been Catholic here for a long time. I forget how many years. The first time the missionaries came it was August 5th. Quite a few years ago we started having 5th of August, big

42

celebration. During the weekend we have races, ball games, dances and stuff like that. Other religions try to come in here. I think it's a waste of their time. I don't think anybody would turn away and join them. Everybody in town is Catholic. Their religion is strong.

Father Baud was here about thirty years. The last six or seven years he used to have dances for the young people. Try to keep them out of mischief. Every night, Monday to Friday, seven to nine-thirty. We paid a quarter to come in. That quarter they used to buy the games. Monopoly, Parcheesi, checkers, dominoes. Then once a week dance. Father Baud started to learn to dance too.

One thing I remember when I was growing up was Stickdance. Father Baud, our most favorite missionary, was very much

Daniel Sipary, Father Jetté with camera and Andrew Johnson in Nulato.

against Stickdance. We had no Stickdance for maybe fifteen years. Father used to preach against it. We would put up a stick in the center of the hall and dance around it. He thought we were adoring the stick. But no, we just do it for fun.

I cannot express it, but we put up the Stickdance for the dead people. It's to pay the people that help bury our dead. You pick out someone that you think did the most. A lot of times you can't remember who did the most during someone's death because you are grieving. You don't even pay attention. So you have to ask other people. Like who bought the lumber for the casket. You pick out that person and dress that person to more or less thank him. Or you dress people that helped make boots, gloves, mittens, cap, or help buy clothes. You just give them these little gifts. That's what the Stickdance is for.

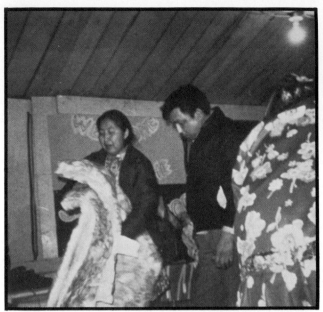

Josephine and Simeon Mountain at the 1976 Kaltag Stickdance.

Finally the Bishop said it was okay to have the Stickdance. There's only two places in Alaska that have it. Kaltag and Nulato. When the Bishop first say okay we started having it same year. One in Kaltag and one here. It didn't work out too good. People couldn't afford to fly to two Stickdances in the same year. Especially from Fairbanks or Anchorage. We even had a person from Rome come to the last two Stickdances. That's a long way. So we made agreement that Kaltag have one year and Nulato will have it the next year. It started working a lot better.

Simeon Mountain surrounded by singers and dancers at the 1983 Nulato Stickdance.

We have good singers and some lively songs in Nulato. I remember in my Grandma Mary, Grandpa Charlie and my other Grandpa Jack Patsy's days, people were against them. The teenagers, the people my age now. The Stickdance lasts a week. Starts on Monday and ends Sunday. The old people used to sing till maybe two o'clock every night during Stickdance week. The kids in my age used to talk against my grandpa and grandma. Call them names. They were against the singers because they wanted to modern dance. Waltz, foxtrot, one-step, square dance, things like that. They wanted violin and guitar. Then that twist came along.

A few years ago it turned around. Now the teenagers and even younger want the Indian singing. A lot of the young ones dance during the Stickdance week. I don't know what caused it but it just turned completely around. Everybody wants Indian singing. I'm happy to see it. I enjoy it too. Although I don't have the voice to sing and I don't know any songs anyway.

A lot of the songs that they're singing are the songs my grandma and grandpa Mountain made. My grandma used to

Dancing at the 1983 Nulato Sitckdance.

Dancing around the pole at the 1983 Nulato Stickdance.

45

make song in one afternoon. She start thinking of a song. Soon she start humming it. Pretty soon she put the words together and she's got a song. We have some young people now, people my age, that made song. Pauline Peter, Tassie Saunders, Sebastian McGinty, they made few new songs. But lot of these songs are made maybe seventy years ago and they're carried on down.

Fred Stickman told me ten years ago that we started to twist before White man. I think people used to be crazy for Stickdance long time ago, is because it's twisting type dance. People go out there and twist and sing with it. You have to sing. Otherwise it's hard to dance. Fred is right. If you see a Stickdance, you see we started twisting before White man.

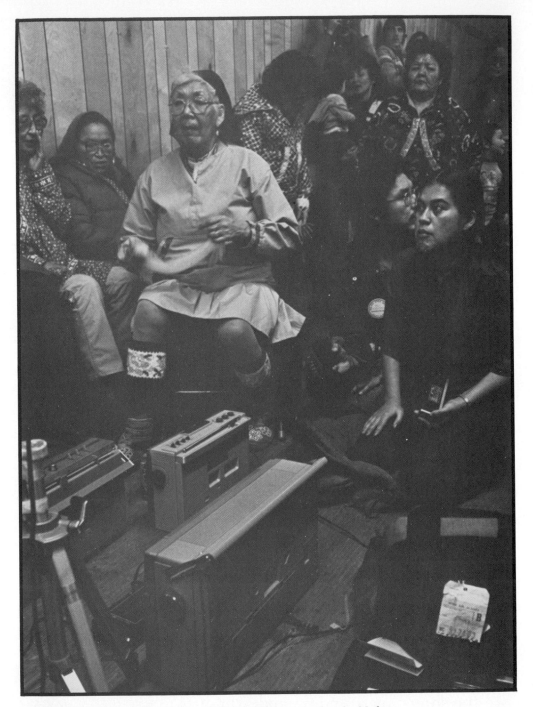

Tassie Saunders leading the 1983 Stickdance singing in Nulato.

46

Pauline Peter singing at the 1983 Stickdance while others listen or dance along.

Singers at the 1983 Nulato Stickdance. L-R: Sebastian McGinty, Clemmet Esmailka, Romeo Stickman, Tassie Saunders dancing and Simeon Mountain.

47

Chapter Four: Military, Postmaster, and Lowball

Out of the Village

I quit school when I was seventeen to help my uncle and aunt. Mostly I was cutting wood, getting in water, hauling wood, helping my uncle in fishing and things like that until I was inducted into the army. I went through basic at Ft. Rich near Anchorage during Christmas 1952. There I went to Ladd Field, Ft. Wainwright now, and stayed there the rest of the time. Twenty-one months in a heavy motor company.

When my friend Ray Ambrose and I went in for our physicals it was the first time we traveled out of the village. Nobody told me what to do. Right now I admire these kids going on field trips with people. They learn what to do.

Our first experience in Fairbanks we went into a restaurant. I sat down on a chair along the counter. Ray sat next to me. I just waited for the waiter. I didn't know what to do. I didn't know there was such a thing as a menu. I didn't know you could order. Ray didn't know what to do either. Pretty soon I see him reaching out in front where there was salt and pepper, napkins, sugar and things like that. He pulled out this funny thing. It looked like a book.

"We're supposed to look at this," he tell me.

I open it up and see all the things we can order. I thought

right away to myself I guess I should look down the list and tell the waiter what I want. Then they'll cook it that way, I guess. Right away I try to pick out something. When the waiter came she wouldn't wait too long for me to put in my order. I had to say it right off. It was my first experience. I didn't know we were supposed to order.

Another time on the same trip I went to a movie. It was a double feature and all during the movie I wanted to go to the bathroom. Halfway through the first movie I got real restless. I didn't know there was a bathroom in the building. I thought there were bathrooms only in hotels. So I had to wait. See. No one told me. All I would have to do is go into the lobby and ask someone where the closest bathroom was. Something like that. I didn't know. What a relief after I got back to the hotel.

Another problem was money. I had money in the First National Bank but I didn't know how to get it. On the way home I ran out of money. The army was sending us home after the physical and we stopped in McGrath on the way to Galena. It was evening, suppertime. We followed the rest of the passengers into this hotel. Pretty soon they all started sitting around this table. It was all set. My buddy Ray wouldn't come. He had no money either so he wouldn't come. He was staying in the lobby. Once in a while he looked at me and he laughed. Even he was hungry. Reaching in his pocket telling me you have to pay, you know. I didn't pay no attention to him and I started eating. You didn't have to order. Everybody had the same dish. I thought the airline was paying for it. Pretty soon they came by with meat and potatoes. Serving us. I just started eating. Pretty soon the same waiters were coming around with a little piece of paper. Giving a little piece of paper to everybody. I looked at it. A bill for three or four dollars!

It spoiled my meal. I was only half way through but I couldn't eat no more after I saw that bill. So I went over to the cashier. I guess she was the owner of the hotel. I told her, "I have no money. I have no money to pay for the meal. But I have money at home. I could send you money. I'll send a check. Will you give me your address?"

"Oh," she says, "you don't have to pay. That's okay."

I told her I thought the airlines was paying that's how come I started to eat. She said again I didn't have to pay, but I was too bashful to go back in to the table and finish.

It was hard to get adjusted to military life. The hours, the discipline, the food. Hard to get adjusted. But you met some nice friends. And some others not so good. I got along with everyone.

We could go to school in the army but I didn't go. They had a school for anything you wanted to take up. But the school was at night. At night and on the weekends. So I didn't go. I wanted the evenings and weekends to myself. I wanted to go to the movies or just go downtown or go to Nenana for the weekend.

Leadership School

Leadership school was mandatory. You had to go. It lasted for thirty days teaching you how to run men, how to give classes, and stuff like that. Three months before I was getting out of the army and they wanted to send me to the school. I told the company commander I'm going home in three months what good would it be to send me to leadership school? I told him I was too dumb. I couldn't learn anything. It wouldn't do any good to send me to school.

"The whole company is talking about you," he told me. "We're all talking about you because you're a corporal and you never went to leadership school. We've been sending privates and pfc's. You're supposed to go. And what you learn up there will help you even in civilian life.

50

So I said I'd try. Then he called me by my first name and said, "Would you hang a man for trying?"

"No sir," I said.

"Same way with me," he said. "You go up there and you try. If you get kicked out because you can't learn anything, I'm not going to bust you. I might even promote you to sargeant."

The school was in Eielson Air Force Base twenty-six miles away. I remember going up there in a jeep. I kept looking at the road and the door. I was going to make it some way so that door was going to open and I would accidently fall on the road. Hopefully I would end up in the hospital with not too many broken bones for two or three weeks. By then it would be time for me to get out and go home. Anyway, thank God I didn't do that.

At Eielson we went up two flights of stairs into a building. A sign above the door said, "The Best Men in the World Pass Through These Portals" or something like that. My heart was just about ready to quit. We went inside and signed in. They started giving everyone supplies. We got sheets and blankets.

We went back at night and they started giving us manuals. One, five, six, nine, ten, eleven, twelve. Thirty-three manuals! I could barely hold the stack! I look at him, "how am I going to read all of this?" We brought them back to the barracks and put them in the locker. In order, by the numbers, in the military manner.

We had different subjects like map reading, patrolling, weapons, and things like that. Every three or four days we would take a test. The scores were posted on the bulletin board and I would be number ten or twelve. There were sixty of us at first. Twenty got kicked out so that left forty to finish.

It was a real strict school. Thirty demerits and you got kicked out. And a demerit was any little thing. A button not buttoned. Your belt

51

buckle over too much to one side not right in the middle. Your clothes not pressed. Your shoes not shined enough. When you put the shoes you're not wearing under your bunk they have to be laced up and even. If one shoe is a little too far out you get a demerit. Any little thing.

I remember sometimes we'd give a display of our mess kit. We'd put it on our bunk. They had a diagram that they changed around. If a spoon is not in the right place according to the diagram, you get a demerit. Your hair not combed. A little dust under you bunk. Anything. Five demerits during the week and you couldn't go to town for the weekend. I used to go to town every week and I never got kicked out.

I had to give a five minute talk, a fifteen minute class on company duties, and two fifty minute classes. They critique your five minute talk for things like if you look at only one person, pace around too much, or if you stand in one place, or if you jingle money in your pocket, or play with your dog tags while you're talking. They grade you on that. At graduation I was eighteenth out of forty so I didn't do too bad. And most of the others were high school or college students.

Coming Home

December 9, 1954, I got out of the army and came home for good. My pay plus my soldier's deposit came to $750. I bought a chain saw and a radio. For the first four or five days when I started up the chain saw everybody used to gather round. Zing! It cut lots faster than swede-saw or two-man saw. I was about the first person to have a chain saw here. I kept it going so long people laughed at it. It had homemade parts out of wire and string, even nails. I still have it in the cache somewhere.

Coming back to Nulato was even harder than leaving. Getting

adjusted all over again. For a while there was just like nothing to do. So I just laid around. Help around the house a bit. Haul wood, cut wood, pack it in. Getting water. And we put in a fish trap. That was one of the last years we put in a fish trap. After a while I went trapping with my cousin Herman Silas fifteen miles up towards Kaiyuh.

Max Hundorf, Sr. was postmaster and recommended my Uncle Dan take over for him. Max was retiring so they had to get someone else. Then my Uncle Dan got sick. He had a sore lump on the back of his neck that wouldn't heal. He had to go to the hospital. The three leaders in the community got together — Father Baud, Max Hundorf, Sr. and Uncle Dan to pick another officer-in-charge for the post office. They chose me.

I told them no. I'm young. I want to go travel. I want to go to other villages when there's good time. I don't want to be tied down. I been tied down all my life. I never tried living. I was forbidden when I was a teenager to go to Koyukuk, Kaltag, or Galena for any good time or funerals or anything. Then I was stuck in the army for two years and now I want to be free.

They said take it for a little while until we find someone else. I thought I'm too dumb. I couldn't learn how to run the post office. "Sure you'll learn," Max told me. "You're not going to be young all the time. It's better than

Simeon's post office desk at the back of his home in Nulato.

53

beaver trapping and you're right in the house. You don't have to go out in the cold. In the summer you don't have to work outdoors in the rain to make a living. You can make a comfortable living working in the house playing postmaster.'' Finally I said I'd do it for a while. Try it.

The last day before he quit he gave me two hours instruction. Then he told me if I get stuck to look in the books, look at his work, and figure it out. The first couple days weren't easy. April 1, 1955, I took over the post office and the next January I got my official commission as postmaster from Postmaster General Arthur Summerfield.

The post office has changed quite a bit since them. We used to haul the mail back and forth from the airport by wheelbarrow. All the way up the hill, towards the graveyard and up on the ridge. We didn't have this road straight up the hill in those days. On a rainy day it was really hard. Pushing that wheelbarrow and no traction under you. You keep sliding back.

We had no communication those days. No radio. The plane schedule was ten o'clock in the morning but

sometimes you'd go up there and wait all day long. Come back seven or eight o'clock at night. And just when you're around the bridge, here comes the plane. So you have to walk back up the hill pushing the wheelbarrow. Mosquitoes biting your arms and neck all over. Nothing to eat all day.

The catalogs are the ones that used to make me cry. Sears Roebuck and Montgomery Ward catalogs. You know how thick they are? And sometimes seven or eight bags full. They used to make me sweat. Now I go in the truck. Turn the key and you're up the hill in no time.

More Business

Up until four or five years ago the post office was fourth class. That meant the government didn't supply any support like an adding machine. I had to supply everything I needed from paper clips to mail boxes. Everything we needed to work with. I started with $98 in the cash box every two weeks and that was my pay. I paid myself every two weeks and by Wednesday of the second week I'd have to start holding back money so there would be a hundred dollars or so there by Friday.

We got paid for the money orders we issued too. In the early days we got a cent and a half for each money order. So in a quarter, three months, I used to pay myself five or six dollars for issuing money orders. We didn't make out very many orders in those days because there was less money and the stores brought money into town from the bank. That way cash could circulate. But now the stores don't

Simeon at work in the post office 1982.

Simeon Mountain, Jake Seppla and Ella Vernetti. "We did a Stickdance aboard the Beach Combers at Kodiak." 1970.

bring in cash. Everything is money orders here now.

People come to the post office with a check and they buy money orders to pay the store bill or whatever. Or they come to the post office with a money order to make another. I deduct it and give them a money order for the balance. So it's just check and money orders exchanged. Hardly no cash going around. My boss doesn't like the idea. A lot of times he tell me not to cash checks. We do not take checks for the purpose of cashing it because we're not a bank. But what can we do? So I have to be personally responsible for the checks. If it is no good, I'm the one who is going to end up paying for it. I've had a few bounce, but it was all made good later. I didn't have to wait long.

Four or five years ago our rating went up. We were doing more business. That business is created by the number of money orders and stamps we sell. The more business we do, the more stamps and money order fees we advance, the higher our rating. So now we get support from the government. We have a money order machine, adding machine, and I could have a telephone if I wanted it.

Gambling

After three or four years I started liking being postmaster but even now I get disappointed with it a lot of times. Like the other night they were playing cards up there. Lowball. I love to gamble but I had to quit early. I have to get up about a quarter to seven and be working at eight. Sometimes I don't like it, but there's no choice. If I was not the postmaster I would have to do something else for a living.

A lot of people around here play lowball. Gambling. In the same card game you play deuces wild, high or low split, ace king spit in the ocean, and three or four others. Lowball is usually when people come from other villages but we play pan every night. Same group of people always come to that. It's entertainment for older people. You should have nine for a game but you can have three or four. Not much money is involved. The other night when there were a lot of people from different villages and with firefighting and everything there was a lot of money. And the bets were pretty high. I played that night for a little while. I won $184 in a couple of hours. I think the game lasted sixteen hours straight through.

Usually now most of the gambling is during death. Because a lot of people come from other villages with money. And during Stickdance. Some people have a lot of money you know. But that's about the only two times. Not much gambling during weddings because people come from nearby villages on the wedding day. Wedding evening they have a dance and reception and next day they all go home.

I'm known as a good gambler but it's just luck. Once in Fairbanks I lost $900 in a big game. Had to put $200 on the table to get into the game. Here we play $5. Josephine was with me. She got so mad. It's all how the cards go. I had only a joker. I drew four cards and made a sixty-four. Only one hand can beat you which is a fifty-four. I won the pot. I didn't have enough to bet all the way. The part I won I stacked up in front of me. Ten hundred eighty dollars. In one pot. I felt real good. Then to show how the cards run, a few hands after that I was going with one, two, three, four and one card to draw. I'm the last man to bet. The first man to bet after the draw laid down a thousand dollars. This other guy called him. I'm sitting there the last man to bet and going with the best cards. I catch another four. No good. You can't have pairs in lowball. And just a few hands before I drew four cards and made a sixty-four. So, no matter how good of a player you are or how good you might know the game, it just take luck. One night you win and the next you lose.

The first time I start seeing gambling was in my army days. I didn't know nothing about gambling. I see them playing lowball in one corner of the building. In another corner of the building they're playing 4-5-6. I see them throwing dice. Another place they're playing a game they call blackjack. Another place they're playing another game again.

I see them betting ten, twenty dollars. I see them throwing dice and hear "ace away" and then somebody grabbed the money. I used to stand and look at them and say, "How do they enjoy themselves betting twenty dollars and rolling the dice and acing away?" I didn't see how the heck they could enjoy themselves. That's not for me I used to say. Dress up, slick up, go downtown. Here I end up being one of the worst ones. Love to gamble.

Taxi Service

Besides being postmaster, we work for Galena Air Service and run a cab service. We have two radios supplied by Galena Air. When people come we call the planes and Galena Air gives us a certain percent. It isn't very much but it helps a little.

After we got involved in that, the man at Galena Air wanted me to start a cab service. I had been driving before. If you notice the old truck by the bridge, I used to own most if it. All old trucks. So I thought of it for a while. Running a cab. People were always bothering us for transportation so he told me to get a license and do it legally.

I went to the police and got an Alaska State

Post office in Nulato at the Mountain's home, 1982.

58

Driver's Manual to study. Then I went to Galena to take the test and I didn't make it. But I remembered the questions so when I came back to Nulato I studied those ones I didn't know. You can try again after two weeks. Turned out it was lucky I studied the whole book because the second time the questions were all different. I passed that time. Then I asked the Council for permission to run a cab service and they were very happy about it.

At first people were reluctant to pay. Maybe people would talk about it and maybe they would expect a free ride. I would tell them a dollar and a half a piece and they weren't used to it. Till finally they got used to it and now they don't mind. It's just like going into a store. You get a loaf of bread you have to pay for it.

Before last year I used to break down a lot with my old trucks. People used to get disappointed. Not at me, but on account of the truck, you know. They know they would have a hard time getting a ride from other people because they're not around. Us, we're around most of the time.

Now we charge two dollars to go out the hill to the airport with a four dollar minimum. We don't make much but the little we make helps. I think there'll be more business when most of the people move back to the new townsite, but I don't know if I want to be involved in taxis, provide taxi service back there. There just isn't much money it it.

National Guard

We're talking about making another National Guard battalion just for the Interior. I'm one of the four First Sargeants in the battalion we have now. This next month will be a big recruiting drive. If we get enough men and women I would probably be the Sargeant Major. I saw a note on my record signed by the battalion commander that Simeon would be very hard to beat for the next Sargeant Major. It's a coveted position already.

Nulato is the headquarters of Company D. We're made up of people from Huslia, Nulato and Kaltag. Also Koyukuk, Galena, Ruby, Hughes and Allakaket. Last year they gave award plaques and we won them all. This year they did it too but we lost to Company B. I think the battalion commander gave it to B in order to treat people equal or not to have too much friction between companies.

We get quite a few benefits for being in the National Guard. We can fly National Guard aircraft anyplace between the villages if they're going around here. We have Commissary and PX privileges and life insurance. After you retire there's more. You can go anyplace around the world on military aircraft on space available. You can go to any armed forces hospital and you can see a dentist. You could borrow up to $80,000 for a house and up to $120,000 to start a business. We get paid for drills too. It goes according to your time and grade. On a weekend you can make anywhere from $13.50 to $50.00 a drill depending on your rank. We do five drills on a weekend.

Drills are on different subjects like map reading, first aid, patrolling and weapons. Almost every year we fire our weapons and have weapons qualifications. Now we've got a machine for training that shows pictures and has a tape to go with it. It's very interesting. Much easier to learn and much easier on me the instructor.

First Sargeant Simeon Mountain and Major Cardwell with the National Guard in Nome, 1979.

Simeon Mountain Collection

Chapter Five: Life Is More Comfortable

Married to Josephine

Josephine was working in Tanana when I first met her. She was passing through Nulato in April and she ate with us. My Auntie Jessie is her cousin so she invited her for supper. I remember I glanced at her and to myself I said, "I wonder if she'd be my wife." And I glance at her again. "No, I don't think so. No . . . I think I look for someone else." I thought, you know. That was all.

Next time I saw her was in May or June. She came to see my friend, Ray Ambrose. That was her boyfriend. She came down to see him. But I guess it's God's will he was in Kaiyuh and she ended up in my house one evening. She had just started to drink. She never drank all her life and just a few months before that we start hearing people saying she started to drink. That was news. Big news. Headlines.

She was 19 or 20. Some girls started drinking even earlier. You hear about it. A young girl passed on stuff. So she started to drink two or three months before that and she was drinking that evening. We started visiting, talking. Soon before we knew it it was four or five o'clock in the morning. That was all. We never did anything funny. Or even asked to see her again. She went back to Tanana the next day. And her boyfriend was still in Kaiyuh. Then we started to write to each other.

L-R: Magdalen Silas, Irene Solomon, Josephine Mountain and Anna Madros, 1948.

I don't know who wrote first but we were answering each other right along. We just fell in love I guess. July she quit to help her mother fish in Kaltag. That's when I borrowed my uncle's inboard boat to go see her on weekends. Not bad going down but a slow five or six hours coming home. Around first of August I asked her to get married. She said okay so we went to see Father Baud.

He had to make announcements. Three announcements in those days. Now I think it's down to two. On Sunday during Mass he would say so and so want to get married does anyone have an objection. August 22, 1958 we got married.

We had a big wedding and got lot of gifts. I had my own house already then. I figured it would cost so much for rent and just a little more for labor so the sooner I built my own house I would be that much ahead. My Uncle Romeo Stickman got me the logs.

Life is Beautiful Without Alcohol

It's different being a teenager now than when I was young. We never used to drink so much right out in the open. Of course there was no dope. And people never used to live with each others. Now it looks like people live with each other two, three years. Sometimes they live with each other, sometimes they get married. There used to be teenage drinking I remember. I never did drink much in those days, but I remember a few instances.

When I was about fifteen, we had a liquor store here. A pint was about three dollars. Three or four of us used to get in together and get an older person to buy a pint for us. We'd give him a drink to pay him. Then we'd drink the rest together. I remember doing that two times.

Once there were three of us. Went in together to buy a pint and we finished it while we were standing up. Just pass the bottle round and round. Take one drink and pass it. Maybe we finished that pint in five minutes.

I went home to my Uncle Dan's house and went straight to bed. I just start sweating. I remember my uncle saying, "Gee, what's the matter with him? Wonder how come he went to bed so early without making shavings or drinking milk or anything?" They never found out.

Another time we went in together and got one old man to get a pint for us. We passed it to him to take a drink and before he passed it back, in one swallow, he drank two-thirds of the pint. We had only a little bit for all of us. That was all. After that I never drank for a long time.

One of the things that really helped was I heard my Uncle Dan telling another person that he heard Leo Demoski saying, "Simeon is nobody's fool." Pertaining to drinking, you know. Well, I said to myself, if that's the way my Uncle Dan thinks I'll just be nobody's fool. I never drank. Till I got in the army.

Over a two year period, first I started with one beer on Saturday night. Nothing on Sunday or during the week. By two years later, I still wouldn't go over three or four beers on a whole Saturday night. Only after I got married I start drinking. I start drinking a lot. Finally I quit once because I beat up Josephine.

I didn't know about it. One morning I woke up, we were living in the old house then. The sun was shining in the house.

Early in the morning. It was beautiful outdoors. I had a headache, I had to get up. I had to work. Got up and walked halfway across the house and I see her bra in the middle of the floor. I must have beat her up I thought. I went over and looked at her face. She was still sleeping. But no . . . no marks on her. "Well," I told her, "get up, I want breakfast." And she says to me, "Cook for yourself!"

"What happened?"

"You beat me up last night. Lucky I protected my face."

I looked at her. Lots of bruises. All blue. Then I say, "I quit. I wouldn't drink no more." She jumped up right there. I don't know how she believed me. "I'll cook for you."

So she cooked for me and I just quit drinking. Then I started again in about five or six years. I started again and

Josephine in front of the Mendenhall Glacier. "She went with me to the postmaster's convention in Juneau, 1959."

Simeon Mountain and Ivan Sipary hauling water with a Ranger in Nulato, 1975.

little by little I fell back again into the same pattern. Even worse over a seven to ten year period. At the end I started passing out around the table every night. I wake up in the morning in bed. Work all day. Couldn't wait till five o'clock. Five o'clock comes, start drinking again. Got to where I was drinking one quart every day. One quart whiskey. Then I got into another accident and it taught me.

It was June 26, 1973. I remember the day so good. I went up the hill in the ranger. Going up to the runway. Instead of going on the road all the way to turn around I made a shortcut. I guess the bank was too steep. And there was a lot of people in the trailer. I know there was four of us on the truck, on the ranger itself. We did a somersault and it landed on four of us. We all ended up in the hospital. I had to stay for three weeks, but the others weren't hurt so bad. My chest was all crushed.

Josephine was in the hospital that time too for something else. She got out about a week ahead of me. That first day in the hospital I was wondering how I'm going to make it after five o'clock. I wonder if I'll live? I had gotten to where at five o'clock I have to have a drink. Five o'clock came and I just feel myself, touch myself. Seeing if I was living, I guess. I don't know. To see how I felt on the inside. I wanted a drink. Six o'clock. Seven o'clock. And so the night passed. I was living.

Same way the next night and the next night. After two weeks I was still craving for drinking, but it went away a little. I wanted to come home before Josephine and empty all the little caches I had here and there. Bottles. Some a little bit, some more. Some full ones, some half full. Here and there. Different places I had bottles cached. I wanted to get home first

Josephine Mountain, Rhonda Patsy and Pamela Esmailka reading catechism in Nulato, 1976.

and throw them all out. And try to stay away from it for a while anyway.

When I came back, Josephine was home ahead of me. The first chance I got that evening, when she was not looking, I look here and there . . . everything was all cleaned out. I didn't find one bottle. I never mentioned anything. Never mentioned one thing.

For a month after that I used to moan. Work all day in the post office and when it's time to go to bed, I'd just start moaning. It hurt inside from being crushed. Ribs broken, my shoulder dislocated. When it's time to go to bed I'd just start moaning. It hurt. She'd look at me. "I wonder if he'll ever drink again after all that suffering." That was a little over six years ago and I haven't touched a drink except by accident.

We were over in Rome. I took a bottle to pour water and it was wine. I couldn't read the Italian writing. They always serve you wine with your meals. Free. We just leave it there, never drink it. Though I made the mistake with this one. I poured it in my cup and it bubble up. The water bubble up over there too so you can't tell the difference. I drank it. Took a big swallow of it. Here it was wine. Tasted good. I told Josephine that was wine. She said, drink it. So I drank it with my supper. Felt bum for two days.

Coming back from New York to Seattle on the same trip I had about four or five glasses of champagne. I sure wanted them that time. But Josephine kept looking at me with the side of her eye so I had to quit. I haven't drank since and I hope I never drink again.

I live a lot better. I'm happier. I don't have to wake up in the morning and think to myself, gee, I wonder what I did last

66

night. Try to put things together. Gee, I wonder if I did something wrong? I wonder if I scolded someone. Might have hurt someone. So I'm scared all day till about noon. If I never hear nothing by then, I said, well, I guess I didn't do anything. Now I don't have to worry about things like that.

My daughter Marie got married last August in Koyukuk. I had to give a speech. No one else to talk. It's no good when someone doesn't say anything. Any special occasion. Funeral or marriage. Potlatch. Some kind of award or anything. When people get together like that and no one says

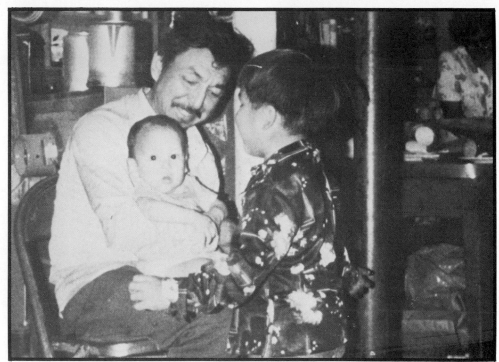

Simeon Mountain with grandson Charles and "My Boy Cutes", 1979.

anything it's no good. It's sad, they say, you know, in Indian way, they say *K'ilahdoyk'ilik hoolaanh* which means it's sad when someone doesn't say anything so I made a speech. I thanked the people for coming to Marie's wedding. They gave her a lot of gifts. I thanked them. Toward the last part of the speech, I directed it toward Marie and David. I closed telling them a little sentence that I saw in a magazine. *Life is beautiful without alcohol.* Everybody was real happy. They say that was the best speech they heard for a long time. But life really is. I hope I don't drink again.

A lot of dreadful things happen during drinking. A lot of people cry. Lot of tragedies. Losing a lot of young people that wouldn't have happened if they were sober. There's quite a few lose their life one way or another. We had quite a few shootings. Young people. Fortunately, we have four from around here that shot themselves and are still living. But it still didn't teach them, they'll go back to the same way.

When I was young I don't remember losing young people to alcohol. Here within the last few years we've had five or six self-inflicted wounds that were fatal. Alcohol related. I don't know why. Life is much easier for them now than in our days. Easier to get things. Food and everything. Life is more comfortable. Electricity, freezers, things like that.

Kris Ann Mountain and Charles, 1979.

Get a Good Education

People just vote for me to be on the Community School Committee (CSC). I never ran. Even the teachers come by and encourage me to run again after my term is up. I've been the president of our committee for three or four years now.

My biggest hope for my children is for them to get a good education. I'm having a hard time getting grants for them to go to college. Not only grants, I seem to be discriminated against on account of my job. My children have a hard time even to get

Josephine, Paul and Simeon Mountain at Paul's 1980 graduation.

68

Youth Corps jobs. I see other kids whose parents make just as much as I do and more, but because I'm postmaster and I have steady income, my children have a hard time.

I remember a few years ago when Kris Ann just finished high school someone came down from Fairbanks. They had three or five thousand dollars for some kind of program in Nulato for girls who were going to college to work. Sixty days, something like that. He came to hire ten girls. We heard about it and Kris Ann went down and asked. They wouldn't take her. The next morning I got up early and I brought her back down. This person had nine girls waiting outdoors. One more. So he goes to wake up another girl. He made two or three trips before the girl came down. The tenth one. So I told Kris Ann, "Let's go home."

On our way home, around the church down here, I glanced at her and I saw tears coming down out of her eyes. I looked away, pretend I didn't see her. After we went back into the house, I told her, "You have to go to college. That's the only way you can get a job around here. Got to have more schooling. You can't get a job because you are the postmaster's daughter. I want you to finish college."

Never Go Back

We'll never go back to the old ways. Like from the chain saw to the swede saw. Same way with the wheelbarrow. I'd never go back to the wheelbarrow. One of my cousins told me, "If there start being roads, I'll bet you're the first one to buy a truck." Sure enough I was one of the first ones. I think we went through five or six.

And building houses. We used to auger the holes by hand. Now all we do is put the auger at the end of a drill and just press down a little. It save you time, build your house faster. If you pay for labor, it's cheaper. Life is just much easier by electricity. By the time our children are older there will be other changes too. In tools and stuff. Make it a little easier for them.

Some things change too fast though. Like with Land Claims. I have a hard time understanding all the things that go with Land Claims. I hear people that are involved in it saying that sometimes it's hard for them to understand too. Young people don't seem to even think about it. They just take it for granted.

Simeon Mountain Collection

I'm really surprised at my children. They know more about world affairs and stuff like that than when I was their age. They tell me things they hear on the radio. They get really excited about the World Series. About football games. About NBA, pulling for the Sonics.

Simeon's daughter Marie at home in Nulato, 1979.

Even the election. National election. Anxious to see who's going to be the next president. Who's going to be next governor. The children these days are more exposed to the news media than we were. I'm sure other children around town are the same. It really gives me a thrill to see my little boys, Erick, asking who I think is going to be next president. Or who I'll pull for in the World Series. Or NBA. Or football.

Nulato 1982.

Nulato 1982.

Rome

I was about eight or nine years old when I first made up my mind to go to Rome. 1973 was supposed to be Holy Year. The Holy Doors over there open every 33 years. I used to read about Rome all the time. Pope, Vatican City, the Catacombs, St. Peter's Square and all those things. So I made up my mind I was going to go to Rome in 1973. I always used to talk about it. All the way even while I was in the army I said to myself, I was going to keep my promise. So I start saving money. I put a little bit away whenever I could. When I got married I told Josephine about it.

With one year to go we talked about it again. She said, "No, I don't want to go with you."

"Why?"

"Because you didn't promise yourself that you were going to take me when you first made your promise."

"Well," I told her, "I didn't know you were going to be my wife." We talked about it and she finally agreed to go.

We went to Fairbanks that winter for the Winter Car-

Fred Stickman's funeral in Nulato, September 1979.

nival. While we were up there we went to the Federal Building and asked them about getting a passport. We didn't know how to go about it. The clerk said we have to go see a photographer and get a picture taken. We went to a photographer then back to the Federal Building to fill out an application. It cost $48 for the two of us. We got them two or three weeks later in the mail.

We came home and I talked to the station manager in Galena about how we can go about getting to Rome. Then I saw a pamphlet to contact Father Edward in New York. He arranged for me to write to a travel agent. I guess it was all God's will because we got there and we got in a good group. It was $567 each for three weeks from New York to Rome and back. Everything taken care of. All our hotels, bus, guide, tips, meals, all except four or five meals we had to pay on our own. Then it was another $1,000 between here, Anchorage, Chicago, and Washington D. C.

We stayed in Washington D. C. for three days. We went through the Washington Mall, Senate Building and White House. Went to see the Washington Monument, Lincoln Monument and all those places. Arlington National Cemetery. We went to see the Tomb of the Unknown Soldier and we saw them changing guards. Then on to New York to meet our group of 150 other people.

We landed in Brussels, Belgium, changed planes and went to Italy. The first town we went through was Milan. One end to the other. We ended up in Rome.

We saw the Holy Father. There were 30-40,000 of us in the auditorium. The Pope gave his address in Latin or Italian. Seven or eight people translated in one after the other. At the end they start singing the Peter Noster in Latin. Here I was singing it right along and it had been twenty years since I had heard Father Baud sing it in church. Josephine just looked at me she was so surprised.

The trip was good and the food was excellent. The only hard part was the water. It was October, early November, but still it was hot. We had to buy extra water with every meal. It was 300 lira a quart and at that time 100 lira was seventeen cents. The price went up and down. Some days the American dollars used to be worth more so that's the days you want to turn your American money into lira. I never knew that there were other countries that used the dollar. They say dollar for their money too. So I got used to saying American dollar.

At one point we were going to go over the border on swinging cable cars from Italy to Switzerland. But it was too windy. I was disappointed besides being scared. You start at the bottom with twenty-four people in the car. It goes a third of the way up the mountain and you go down to twelve. Then a little farther down to eight. Right at the top to cross you go two at a time. We had to come back down from two-thirds of the way because they said the wind was blowing one hundred miles an hour on top.

We went through the border in a tunnel. They say it is the longest tunnel in the world — 8.2 miles. And there were guards on both sides. Armed guards. Scarey, you know. They come in and check for your passport on both sides of the border. We ate lunch in Switzerland, went through part of France, and back to Italy the same day. Three countries in one day!

We kept going to Tourainne, Florence, Pompeii and Venice. I liked Venice very much. The city is built on the water.

Really a beautiful spot but it was stale water. It smelled.

On the way back to Nulato I bought a case of whiskey for a big party. One of my friends was having an open house so I asked if we could have another open house in his place. They were glad because they were still drinking. We had coffee, cake, booze, wine. A nice party. I told them about part of the trip and how we were glad to be home.

Japan

Josephine and I got picked to be chaperones for a school district trip to Japan. Our boy Paul went along too so three members of our family got to make the trip. Beautiful country. I think it's more beautiful than Italy. But if I had a choice I think I would go back to Italy. The food is better. In Japan the food is a lot different. We almost starved. *Kentucky Fried Chicken* and *MacDonald's* are the only ones that saved us.

Raw whitefish for breakfast, raw salmon eggs for breakfast. And each meal, breakfast, lunch and dinner they have a little table. Each person have his own table. You sit on the floor. And all those kimonos. I counted couple times between thirty and thirty-five different things to eat. On each table. Here at home when we eat three or four different things it's real good. But over there it's a little bit of everything. Only thing that saved us that one day was rice.

Nulato 1983.

Nulato 1983.

The place we were supposed to go to was a real popular city, but it was full so we had to go fifteen to twenty miles away to another place. Kind of remote. Nothing but Japanese there. No elevator. You have to walk up six stories and everybody was eating only rice. About the third day the management found out that they better change the diet or we were going to starve. So they started cooking chicken and meat. But they cook it raw, even chicken! They asked Josephine how to cook it. She told them. After that they started giving us American food. That's the only place we really had a hard time.

Everyplace we went to they were having fall festivals. It's something like the Stickdance. And they almost dance the same way. Goes on every evening for about three or four hours. The whole town shows up in the city squares.

Before I went to one of the dances in the squares, three or four of us went out to a bar to see if it was any different from our way. Pretty soon we saw one man getting up and start dancing with himself. Twisting. Pretty soon another man. Pretty soon we see two men going out and dancing together just like along side of each others. Pretty soon we see a girl alone. Then two girls. Then a boy and a girl. I thought they were crazy. There was something wrong. Some screw loose or something like that in their minds. When we start going to these festivals we find out. They go out there and they dance alone just like when we have Stickdance a lot of people like to dance alone. Like to move their whole body. So here that's what they were doing out in the city squares. They just come out from around there and they go in to the bar and they dance the same way.

In the fall over there, corn is their hot dogs. They have corn stands all over. Broiling it, frying it, anyway you want to cook it. And we see people walking around all evening with a stick through the corn and eating it. There they have so much corn they have it for hot dogs.

This year I got another letter from Father Edward about a second trip to Rome. It is $1700 now. We could go but I'd rather be hunting moose this fall. The only place outside of Alaska we're thinking of going now is the Philippines. Josephine has some trouble with her kidneys and we want to see a healer for her. Harold and Florence Esmailka are going soon so we may go with them. We don't know if a healer could do anything. If not, eventually we'll have to live in Anchorage close to those kidney machines. That would really change our life. We like to be in Nulato.

Dee Stickman riding to work in Nulato, 1982.

Looking towards the Yukon, 1982.

Children playing in Nulato, 1983.

77

Nulato, 1983

Index

Simeon Mountain Family Tree

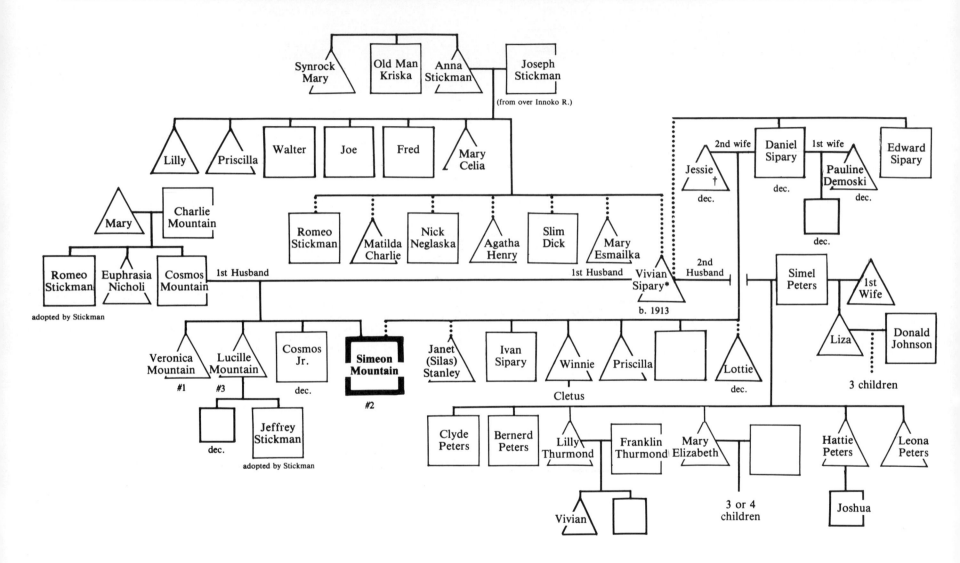

* Vivian's real parents were Mr. & Mrs. Joseph and Olga Onion
† Jessie's parents were Diane and Jack Madros